Raymo's Poems

Raymond Russell

BookLeaf
Publishing

Presentation by *BookLeaf Publishing*

Web: www.bookleafpub.com

E-mail: info@bookleafpub.com

ISBN: 9789395969871

First edition 2022

DEDICATION

Dedicated to my late Mum Evelyn Russell

Some people

Some people are so positive,
And some people are needy.
Some people help others,
And so many others are greedy.
Yet we all have the same values,
As no one really likes pain.
So how can it be possible,
That were not all the same.
Is it in the things that were taught,
In all that we believe.
How could you know,
If you can't even see.
How I feel, or who I am,
As no one told me yours.
So I do have my own plans,
A plan to be happy.
No matter what it takes,
As it is our own choices.
Whether to slither with the snakes,
Or choose just to be you.
Without a second thought,
Knowing how to be happy.
No matter what we've been taught,
As not one of us are stupid.
And I don't believe we are dumb,
I think the problem of today is.
That everyone feels numb,
Scared to be honest.
And say how they really feel,

The thoughts of offending another.
Is becoming so real,
But what we all forgot.
And the thing we need to face,
It may be changed days now.
But we are all the same race,
Humans with love.
Or a human with hate,
There is not a person on this planet.
That finds it difficult to relate,
That things are not right.
This world is in a mess,
Full of anxiety.
And so full of stress,
And it breaks my own heart.
Because I know that it's true,
As I can see it in me.
And I can see it in you,
So let's make today.
The day that we all change,
As looking at the past.
Will just get us all the same,
That same that you either miss.
 or maybe even hate,
It's time to move on.
Again I think we can all relate,
As we only have one life.
So please just be you,
As your Life is as precious.
As I believe mine can be too.

Mother's passing

Such a beautiful mother,
With the biggest of heart's.
You gave up you're own dreams,
Just to give us all a part.
Of who you are,
In all that you believe.
You taught us to be strong,
And to never ever leave.
The family that you made,
In the thing's for what we care.
To look out for eachother,
And to always be there.
For anyone who needs us,
As you taught us were all the same.
We all might look different,
And all have different names.
But you showed us that compassion,
Should never be in vain.
As love and real sadness,
Runs through all of our vains.
So now that it's time,
For you to take your eternal rest,
You can sleep very well,
Knowing you did do you're best.
As there is nothing I would change,
To have a mum like you.
As with all of your wisdom,
There is nothing we can't get through.

So we will all carry on,
And continue to share your heart.
You will be very missed,
But we won't ever be apart.
Because without you mum,
It just won't be the same.
So I will try my very best,
To withhold all of the pain.
As I loss like you,
is so hard to take.
But you created us all,
So it's our time to make.
You so proud,
Of what you left behind.
To share our hearts,
And to always be kind.

If you speak of the devil

If you speak of the devil,
Then he's sure to appear.
Sitting on your shoulder,
Wispering into your ear.
Telling you the things,
That you don't need to hear.
As he takes all of your light,
Then consumes you with fear.
From all of the things,
That you second guess.

Like making new choices,
Or moving on from the past.
If your stuck in a rut,
Then you won't get far.
So don't listen to the devil,
Because you have another ear.
One with an angel,
Wispering softly and clear.
Giving you hope,
With a sense of worth.
Your a beautiful person,
Since the day of your birth.

But the angel and devil,
Are just the choices we make.
We just don't know until made,
If they will make or break.

The way that we feel,
The things that we hoped.
Will we get what we want,
Or do we just cope.
With what we have,
And where we are.
As the choices you made,
Have got you this far.
But it's not the end,
You have more decisions to make.
Is your life forfilled,
Or does it feel fake.
Only you can choose,
What you want to hear.
From the angel and devil.
That's Wispering into your ear.

Look

Look up at the stars,
Not down at your feet.
Look for that feeling,
That you are trying to keep.
Look for the oceans,
So deep and so blue.
Look for the world,
That is inside of you.
Look for a reason,
Not to be quiet with doubt.
Look for a reason,
Where you can scream out and shout.
Look into your heart,
Just listen to its sound.
Where once you were lost,
You can be now found.
Look at your family,
And the ones that you love.
Remember the things,
That others don't have.
Look just how lucky,
We really all are.
Look, after everything,
We have all got this far.
Look after yourself,
Take care of each other.
The world we all share from,
There won't be another.

Look what can happen.
When you open your eyes,
Look what can happen.
When you reach for the sky's.
Look what could happen,
If we gave what we took.
We all live in a world,
Where you just have to look.

No tears

Dont stand at my grave,
Please don't weep no tears.
I have a new life,
With no more fears.
As im the sun in the sky,
That wind on your face.
I'm the grass that is green,
I'm that warming embrace.
I'm the birds you hear sing,
I'm that feeling in your heart.
We will alway be together,
And never be apart.
When you look to the ground,
Or way up to the stars.
There is nowhere you can look,
Where I won't be far.
So when you cry,
And shed your tears.
Do not lost your hope,
Or feel no fears.
As I may be gone,
But I'm very safe.
I'm in your heart,
That beautiful place.
So keep me close,
For all of time.
But don't weep for me,

As I am fine.
Just remember my smile,
And remember my name.
For then my life,
Won't of been in vain.
So when you think of me,
I don't what you to feel sad.
Never be angry,
Or ever get mad.
Instead think of the moments,
That you cherish the best.
As my life will go on,
With every beat in your chest.
So goodbye for now,
As its my time to sleep.
Within your heart,
I'm there to keep.

Hidden disability

People with a hidden disability,
That no one else can see.
Gets judged more than others,
You can take it from me.
Because if you can't see it with your own eyes,
Then how can it be true.
When the person looks happy,
Not feeling down and blue.
But that is the thing,
About a hidden pain.
As you don't need to see it,
To be able to understand or explain.
That not all people are you,
We all deal with things in different ways.
But judging one another,
Won't get a life that we crave.
As we all think that we're better,
Because we only believe what we see.
Not thinking for a second,
Or taking a minute to believe.
That just because you can't see something,
Donest make it untrue.
Because one day when you're not looking,
Well it could happen to you too.

If we could just talk

I wish we could all talk,
And not just speak.
we could learn from one another,
As we have so much to teach.
With a listing ear,
Or a helping hand.
As none of us really,
Have the life that we planned.
But that doesn't matter,
As from today that's the past.
Its the rest of your life,
That you really must grasp.
Because the past is now over,
There is no turning back.
So look to your future,
And get your life back on track.
As one day at a time,
Is all that you can do.
Stop living for others,
And start thinking about you.
Because what is it you want,
From the life that you live.
For others to just take,
Or for you to help give.
As when it's all over,
And you look back at your life.
Will you be happy with your choices,
Or just be content with the strife.

As we only have one chance,
To make our very own mark.
If not for you own,
Then for someone else's heart.
As that's what really matters,
Well it really matters to me.
So this is not a poem,
Its really more of a plea.
To maybe start understanding,
That we are all not the same.
But every single one of us,
Can feel pleasure and pain.
So if we all stood together,
If we just opened our eyes.
We could all help one another,
Without all of the lies.
Then maybe we could live in peace,
In this world that we call home.
As i can make my own choices,
But you need to make your own.

When it's my time

When my life is over,
I truly only have one dream.
I would love for all of the people,
I have ever spoken to or seen.
To remember the things ive said,
For all to take a piece of my heart.
To share it all together,
So we won't ever be apart.
Because i know that life is tough,
It never goes how we wished.
But thinking about the past,
Or feeling like we have missed.
It won't do us any good,
It's just a waste of our time.
caring what other people think,
Or just pretending that were fine.
Just to be that someone else,
Who we all know we are not.
Just to make others happy,
Why have we all forgot.
To be who we really are,
Or to even shed a tear.
To show how we really feel,
Without having any fear.
As no one is perfect,
I don't care what you believe.
As the life i have chosen,

It comes from what i see.
And this life could be better,
In so many ways.
But you have a different in perception,
When you're counting down the days.
When you lose so many you love,
You do start to see.
That life is more special,
than we all care to believe.
So when it's my time,
and i'm no longer here.
Please live your own life,
without any fear.
Because now is the moment,
It's all in the choices that we make.
But i won't choose to waste my life,
by pretending to be fake.
So i wear my heart on my sleave,
I take life day by day.
I'm happy and i'm greatful,
And i believe in all that i say.

A little bit of care.

Broken hearts and minds can be mended.
With a little bit of care,
Like the feeling of emptiness.
Or the thoughts of despair,
I know that it's difficult.
So hard to see the light,
Wanting to give up.
Losing all of your might,
From the loss of a loved one.
Maybe depression or hate,
There is a million other reasons that people can relate.
It drags you down,
You lose all of your hope.
So don't take this lightly,
As this isn't a joke.
Your feelings do matter,
There is people who care.
We have all been through something,
And wished someone was there.
Its not weak to feel lonely,
Or to feel sad or upset.
We are only human,
So we should never forget.
To take care of each other,
Have a little more compassion.
Say how you feel,

And say it with passion.
Give a helping hand,
Take a little time.
With a little bit of care,
We can help heal the mind.
It won't be easy,
 And it will take time.
But if we stood together,
Its a mountain we could climb.
But again it's just me,
With my little one voice.
We can all make a difference,
If we all made the choice.

Heroin

My name is heroin,
I have many names.
I will destroy your life,
As i poison your veins.
And although im a choice,
You should never make.
Because once you start,
Its my time to take.
As i will take your trust,
I will consume your love.
Because when you look back,
I will be all you have.
You wont see it happen,
As you will be looking for me.
But your friends and family,
They can all see.
But you won't even listen,
Because im in control.
Ive took your heart your body,
Your mind and your soul.
I will creep into your life,
With a promise of hope.
But never believe me,
As I'll start as a smoke.

And when i get a chance,
I will start to wheedle.
And the next thing you know,
You will be injecting a needle.
So here is my warning,
That i want to make clear.
Dont lose who you are,
To the gear you should fear.

Bit of fun

I like to watch,

Jaws, Dirty Dancing, Ghost and Scream,
House on the haunted hill, Heat, The A Team.
Planet of the apes, When Harry met Sally,
Superman, Alf and Maulder and Scully.
Rugrats, Button moon, Scrubs and Fraggle rock,
Batman and Robin, 8 mile, and Step up.
The Decent, Colours, The Hills have eyes,
Spiderman, The Turtles, Vanilla Sky's,
Transformers, Ghostbusters, Dreamcatcher, Traitor,
Karate kid, Armageddon and Drilbit Taylor.
Back to the future, Alian and Predator,
Rocky, He Man, 6th sence and Tremors.
E.T, Superted, Batfink, Dead End,
The house on the left, Il sleep when in dead.
Ransome, Childs Play, Goodfellows, Casino,
Knowing, The Happening, and things with Pacino.
Con Air, Saw, Abduction and yes Halloween,
Titanic, Misfits, Lost and Mr Bean.
The Expendables, Rambo, Don't be afraid of the dark,
National Treasure, Men in Black, The Tooth Fairy,
Onk-Back.
Kiss of the dragon, Kickboxer, Double Team,
Executive Target, Bloodsport, and 13.
There's something about Mary, Teen Wolf, James
Bond,
Friday the 13th, Mad Max, Conan,

Porky's, Scary Movie, Snatch, Trainspotting,
The Ring, Devils Rejects, Sunshine, The Forgotten.
Freddy got fingered, Fallen, Stand By Me,
Mirrors, Horizon, The Dentist and Glee.
The Goodies, Freddy Kruger, The Candyman and
Jason,
The Craft, Fire in the Sky and the Terminator
Salvation.
Undisputed, Face Off, The Cabin in the Woods,
Wrong Turn, or Crank but I need to be in the mood

Imagine

Imagine a new world,
Where nothings the same.
Nothing to fear,
With no one to blame.
Imagine a world,
That is full of respect.
With nothing to hate,
Where we share what we get.
Imagine a world,
Where you don't lose your hope.
No one gets angry,
Where everyone copes.
Imagine a world,
Where love meant all.
Everyone was happy,
And no one would fall.
Imagine a world,
Where pain doesn't exist.
One with happiness,
That's peaceful with bliss.
I guess we all could Imagine,
A million other things.
To make life a little better,
And take out some of the sting.

But what we don't realize,
This world we could have.
With no one with nothing,
No one who would starve.
Because if we all stood together,
If we loved each other the same.
Things could be different,
With no more blame.
As Imagine this world,
Has your very own name.
How would you treat it,
I'm guessing never the same.
But that's the thing about life,
Is that we do all have a choice.
But I'm only here,
With my little one voice.

The wag of your tail

The wag of your tail,
That look in your eyes.
Everyday that I awake,
I feel a new supply.
Of love, of hope,
From a loyal friend.
The one with me,
Until the end.
you know my secrets,
You are always there.
You never judge,
You just care.
You just want love,
and we could learn.
A thing from you,
Like how to yearn.
For the ones we love,
No matter what you do.
You follow me about,
You watch me on the loo.
You keep me safe,
You lay at my feet.
You watch over me,
When I'm asleep.

I could not ask,
For a better friend.
My love for you,
Will never end.
You may be a dog,
But not to me.
It's only love,
That I can see.

A world I wished

A different world,
A brand new place.
Where no one cares,
About things like race.
Where fathers get rights,
and no one lies.
Where hearts don't get broken,
And no one cries.
There are no bullies,
And no one's selfish.
We all work together,
And no one's helpless.
There is no hate,
As everyone's kind.
I know it's a dream,
It's only in my mind.
But just for a minute,
Imagine a world like that.
Where the only thing that mattered,
Was loving someone's heart.
We all might be different,
But there's one thing I'll say.
Compassion can save a life,
If you give it everyday.

If I could make you smile

If I could make you smile,
Enough to forget your pain.
Then you can believe when I say,
It would be my aim.
I try to be understanding,
I try never to judge.
I don't like to hold on to hate,
I won't ever hold a grudge.
No I'm not perfect,
I've never claimed to be.
But just like you,
I can also see.
All of the hate,
The lack of respect.
If you don't try your best,
Then what do you expect.
None of us are special,
As we all feel pain.
We have all been hurt,
By another's game.
But you are not them,
Your allowed to see.
Believe in yourself,
Don't just take it from me.

You have your own life,
You never need to follow.
As other peoples opinions,
Can leave you feeling hollow.
So try to live your own life,
With no worry or care.
And I know it's not much,
But il always be there.
As one day at a time,
Is all we can do.
So give me a smile,
And il give one to you.
Then hopefully one day,
Things will go our way.
Let's not wait for tomorrow,
Let's make it today.

Follow your heart

Follow your heart.
Never surrender your dreams.
Always be truthful.
In the things that you mean.
Say how you feel.
Never second guess.
We could all have more.
But we could all have less.
I know that its difficult.
And can sometimes be hard.
To be your own person.
That is always on guard.
Wondering if your loved
Or even just good enough.
I know it can't be easy.
It can sometimes be rough.
But you are the creater.
Of your very own life.
You don't need all of the stress.
From other people's strife.
You are your own person.
Your so beautiful to see.
Its not other people's opinions.
Of who you should be.

That should make you choose.
Or decide who you are.
As following others.
Won't get you far.
So just be who you are.
Just say how you feel.
As no one wants fake.
We all just want real.
So never be scared.
To be who you are.
Believe it or not.
Your a shining star

It won't take your pain

Alcohol won't take your pain,
No matter what you believe.
Taking drugs can't hide the truth,
To the things that you don't want to see.
It may seem like an easy escape,
To the way that you really feel.
But it just hides you in the darkness,
With no ways to start to heal.
Your friend's and family,
They all do know.
They see you slip,
As you dull your glow.
You have lost your way,
But there is a way back.
As you don't need herion,
Alcohol or crack.
To live your life,
Or be happy and strong.
It's the beating of your heart,
That tells you where you belong.
It's every person you love,
Your family and friends.
You miss out on so much,
As you can't see an end.
But never give up,

As there is always a choice.
You just need to get up,
And start using your voice.
To make that change,
That you really need.
Try to think about others,
Before your own greed.
You have only one life,
There is no second chance.
How would you see yourself,
From an outwards glance.

Waiting in heaven

I was born with no voice.
Not even one breath.
But don't feel bad for me,
As I'm now at rest.
I have no hate,
I was taught no shame.
I may be gone now,
But you still know my name.
I will never have to cry,
I won't ever feel sad.
I will never get used,
Or ever get mad.
Il never get heartbroken,
Or ever get let down.
If you could see me I smile,
As i don't have a frown.
It's you I feel sorry for,
As your left with the pain.
But never feel sorry,
With worry and strain.
I have my wings,
I am very safe.
Il be waiting in heaven,
So keep your faith.
As one day soon,
We will meet again.
Until then my love,
Just remember my name.

Dare to reach

Dare to reach into the darkness,
To pull someone into the light.
Sharing your own compassion,
Could save someone's life.
Just a minute of your time,
Or a second to spare.
To lift someone up,
To relieve their despair.
It doesn't take much,
You just need to listen.
As sharing our hearts,
Should all be all our mission.
Because the anger and hate,
It just won't get us far.
Are you part of the darkness,
Or a bright shining star.
As only you can choose,
Who you want to be.
Listen to your heart,
Don't listen to me.
As I don't have all the answers,
To the things that you feel.
The only world that I know,
Is the one I see to be real.

But that's the thing about life,
No one's the same.
As do I really know you,
Or just know your name.
As we only really show,
What we want others to see.
So that's main the reason,
I can only be me.
So I don't ask you to listen,
Or even to care.
Its only my nature,
That I'm hoping to share.
But I've never felt good,
To look down at another.
My words are not here,
To hurt someone or to smother.
Im just trying to be true,
To the things I believe.
I could never be you,
So you will never be me.
But we all have a choice,
In the things that we love
What we all take for granted,
Another wishes they had.

Last breath

As I listen to your last breath,
Sitting next to your bed.
I asked you so clearly,
 And this is what you said.
Do not be sad,
Or cry for me.
I've had my life,
I am now I'm free.
From all the pain,
I've had my time.
Continue my heart,
And you will be fine.
Be the one,
That the world really needs.
Do not live your life,
Full of greed.
Don't be selfish,
Just try to be kind.
You have the power,
Its within in your mind.
For you to choose,
And you too see.
What will you choose,
Who will you be.

As I've lost my chance,
As I did not know.
This is my last breath,
So all I can show.
Is my last ever words,
Is all you can hear.
So please come closer,
Il whisper in your ear.
Dont waste your life,
As we only have time.
Take my advice,
And you will be fine.
As Its my time to go,
But I will leave you with this.
Please don't waste my dying wish,
As one day soon.
You too will see,
The life I leave.
Please live for me.
As my chance is gone,
I will die with regret.
Just live your life,
Not what others expect.

Choose wisely

You should choose your words wisely,
Or at least be carful who you trust.
As not everyone in your circle,
Is really a must.
Some want to dim your light,
Or pretend to take away your pain.
But they are the same people,
That always complain.
They dont care if your doing well,
Or if you even have good news.
They just listen to take,
When you finally snooze.
As they don't like when your happy,
As you take away their light.
How can a friend really be like this,
When a friend should really fight.
For the things that we care for,
If not even for us.
As we all have our own opinions,
We all believe in trust.
But I guess that's the sad thing about life,
Its not about what I believe.
Or who you think your friends are,
Or how different you are from me.

As none of that matters,
When we do all believe the same.
Its just our egos and selfishness,
That highlights our shame.
So I don't really have anything to say,
That will make anything clear.
I just hate the emptiness that some people fear,
I just want to give hope.
For all that feel lost,
As love should never come.
At anyone's cost.

www.ingramcontent.com/pod-product-compliance
Lightning Source LLC
Chambersburg PA
CBHW060920130726

48001CB00006B/2334